A book for love.

A book for tears.

A book to share.

A book for fears.

But most importantly:

A book for **you and me**

You and Me
by Lena-Marie Plath

Vorwort für „Table of Illnesses"

„Table of Illnesses" beschreibt eine persönliche Reise durch meinen Geist und meine Emotionen. Wenn die Welt verwirrt, alles einen überfordert und man zu irren scheint, so hat die Kreativität mir stets Orientierung gegeben.

Zwischen Liebe und Hass gibt es viele Stationen, ebenso viele wie zwischen Freude und Trauer. Sie sitzen eben nicht beim Dinner nebeneinander, sondern reichen sich das Wasser quer über den Tisch.

Meist gegen Mitternacht, wenn die Welt ruhig schlafen sollte, schaltete ich meinen Laptop ein und schrieb.

Das Klicken meiner Tastatur füllte die Dunkelheit des Raumes, und es fühlte sich so an, als würde mit jedem geschriebenen Wort, Satz oder Absatz ein bisschen mehr Ordnung in meinem Kopf entstehen.

Die Emotionen bekamen eine Form und wurden in einem Gefängnis von Schwarz auf Weiß festgehalten, ähnlich wie bei einem Raubtier hinter Gittern, das man aus sicherer Entfernung betrachten kann.

Gemeinsam mit Lena-Marie Plath schufen wir einen Ort, an dem alle Emotionen Platz finden dürfen.

Selbst wenn einem die Poesie nicht zusagt, kann man viel spüren, wenn man die entsprechenden Illustrationen genauer betrachtet.

Jeder Farbton meiner Gefühlspalette hat und muss einen Platz am Tisch finden, und jeder muss akzeptieren, dass keine Farben schöner sind als die anderen.

Mit diesen Worten wünsche ich eine gute Reise.

Bitte nehmen Sie Platz an meinem **Table of Illnesses**

Prologue for „Table of Illnesses"

"Table of Illnesses" describes a personal journey through my mind and emotions. When the world confuses you, everything seems to overwhelm you, and you appear to be going insane. Creativity has always given me guidance

There are many steps between love and hate, just as there are between joy and grief. They don't sit next to each other at dinner but pass water across the table.

Usually around midnight, when the world should be sleeping peacefully, I would turn on my laptop and write.

The clicking of my keyboard filled the darkness of the room, and it felt as if with every word, sentence or paragraph I wrote, a little more order was created in my head.

The emotions were given a form and captured in a prison of black and white, similar to a predator behind bars that can be viewed from a safe distance.

Together with Lena-Marie Plath, we created a place where all emotions can find their place.

Even if the poetry doesn't appeal to you, you can feel a lot if you take a closer look at the corresponding illustrations.

Every shade of my emotional palette has and must find a place at the table, and everyone must accept that no colors are more beautiful than the others.

With these words, I wish you a good journey and…

Please take a seat at my **Table of Illnesses**

Lena-Marie Plath mit einem Kommentar über
die Illustrationen

Diese Harmonie, dieser Tanz von Wort und Schatten,
offenbart die Tiefe dessen, was deine Seele übermittelt hat.
So mögen sich diese Seiten drehen und sanft zeigen,
die Visionen, die aus dem Herzen fließen.

Willkommen zu einer Reise durch die Gedanken
der Leinwand,
wo jede Illustration, jeder Strich,
die hervorgerufenen Gefühle teilt.

Lena-Marie Plath with a statement about
the Illustrations

This harmony, this dance of word and shade,
reveals the depth of what your soul conveyed.
So may these pages turn, and gently show,
the visions that from heartfelt readings flow.

Welcome to a journey through the thoughts
of the canvas,
where every illustration, every brushstroke,
shares the feelings evoked.

Written by Janus Brodersen

Illustrated by Lena-Marie Plath

Table of Illnesses

Take a seat and enjoy the ride

© 2024 Janus Brodersen
Illustration von: Lena-Marie Plath

Druck und Distribution im Auftrag des Autors:
tredition GmbH, Heinz-Beusen-Stieg 5, 22926 Ahrensburg, Deutschland

Janus Brodersen, Hamburg, Germany.

Kontaktadresse nach EU-Produktsicherheitsverordnung: print.brodersen@gmx.de

Table of Illnesses

A table where every illness has its well-deserved place.

ImSane

My mind is like a water balloon.
It leaks from many ends
and all I am trying to do
with my shaky hands
is trying to get through
the day without letting it burst.

Once a leak is covered up
and the water stops to flow
It'll take a while or longer and I promise
the water will go
and find a "as it seems" undamaged spot
and pushes with all its might until
it will pop.

My mind is like a water balloon.
So colorful to cheer you up,
but while you get distracted by its colors,
no one notices it's about to collapse.

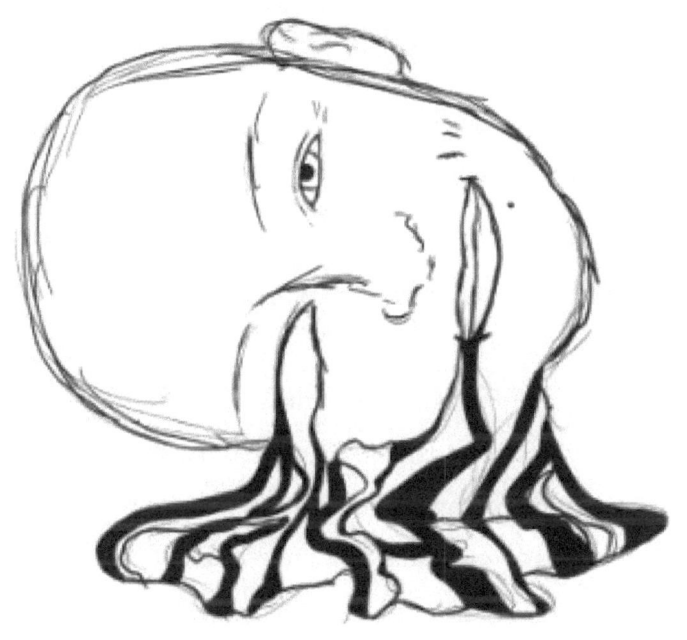

ImSane
by Lena-Marie Plath

Prolonged Grief Disorder

My grief is like an ungifted present.
With pain wrapped around it like ribbons
and the sparks of the candle represent the words
I am unable to say.

The deeper the pain, the wider the love.
The more that I think, the more I will miss.
The way that you sound and the way that you kiss
my pain away when the world was unfair.

Kind of ironic,
you wiped my tears and caressed my cheeks,
kept me going and showed me the way.
Made me smile and life was okay.

But now that I recall you and all that you were,
the pain is rising, and life is not fair,
the clouds are not leaving, and the sky is all grey,
and I have so many words you cannot hear, I'm unable to say.

My grief is like an ungifted present.

With pain wrapped around it like ribbons

and the sparks of the candle that briefly light up the sky

Are the memories I have when I said my goodbye.

Prolonged Grief Disorder
by Lena-Marie Plath

Fatigue

5 more minutes, then I'll go.
Let's skip this task until tomorrow.
We still have time to finish this.
We'll find a time, around later-ish.

If I should, or could, I really would.
I'd finished my doings without a hinder
but I don't feel like doing it right away.
Most days I feel like cinder.

It's like lying underneath a large heavy blanket
that holds me back from resting well.
And fighting to move or break free from the weight
only makes it worse for me to tell.

I am useless,
I am scared.
I am a mess,
Still tried so hard
to stand up and start from scratch.

5 more minutes, then I'll go.

Let's skip this task until tomorrow.

We still have time to finish this.

We 'll find a time, around later-ish.

I am a fair player, but someone else is owning the game.

Fatigue
by Lena-Marie Plath

Broken Heart Syndrome

Dear love, want to feel the rush
get lost in the touch.
Losing ourselves for a minute or two,
And repeat it like we always do.

I wonder if things could change
if they had been written based on love.
I wonder if my sound would vary
if other ears would listen and carry
my voice, my heart, my brain, my soul
across the ocean, far away.
But just by standing still to hear,
does not mean understanding fear.

Love means not being afraid of saying: I do.
Facing your demons and even if you
are laying naked and defeated on the ground,
you still know: I do! An indestructible bond.

Please don't go.
Please don't leave me alone.
I would not be able to function on my own.
Babe, I haven't finished loving you yet.
Do you remember the feel of the day that we first met?

Do you see them spread all on the floor?
Just look between those broken pieces,

let me tell you, there are more.

My offers are small, I won't bring you much.
"Its way cheaper next door" and I am out of luck.
I am biting my nails, and I look like a mess,
my heart has been broken, don't know how to dress.

But I'll promise you,
behind all that coal is shining a star.
It might be small yet, but you can see it way far.
Just take a step closer, just give it a try,
you have to water a plant for it to not dry.

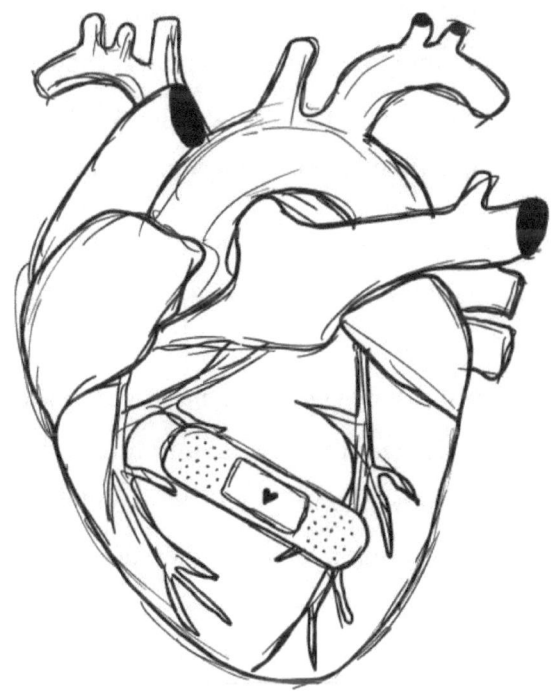

Broken Heart Syndrome
by Lena-Marie Plath

Dysthymia / Deep-Rest

Heaven is a nice place
or why else would people go there for generations.

It must be somewhere between the mountains
that I am too afraid to climb
and the depth I am so worried to dive.

Sometimes I enjoy touching the edge
and just imagine being somewhere instead.
Seeing others suffer from the pain of losing me
and then I notice that honestly…

I like keeping my feet on the ground
and not being able to fly away to the clouds.

Imagine a dance between black and white,
where the music changes the rhythm and intensity of the fight.
Where there is no chance of someone willing to lose
and that's really all they do.

Turning, pushing, twisting, biting and embraced
in a long and loving kiss,

you just blinked for a second and it seemed like you missed

some minutes of the story

but

they switch their rhythm within seconds.

I want people to see how broken I am,

I want people to know how much I cry.

Whilst others listen and enjoy this jam,

I am pouring out my heart, not ready to fly

out from my family's nest, away from home.

Dysthymia / Deep-Rest
by Lena-Marie Plath

Borderline

Isn't it nice to be stuck in between,
like lying inside your sheets with freezing feet and
some birds singing outside while the sun
illuminates your dark painted room.

I always imagined crossing a bridge that was
built across a frozen river with daisies and kids,
playing and chanting and enjoying the sun-
rays that warm up your chest and for a moment it's all gone.

It's like jumping the rope from good to bad,
like swinging from heaven to hell.
A pendulum that sets the mood,
a color plate where every hue is grey.

You don't have to get it, you don't have to care.
You don't have to help me or even spare
a single thought for this situation I am in-
Side: All I want to do is look in the mirror
And say:
"with you I want to spend the rest of my life".

Isn't it nice to be stuck in between,

having the chance of switching the scenes,

being able to feel the heat of the sun,

even though you are not having fun.

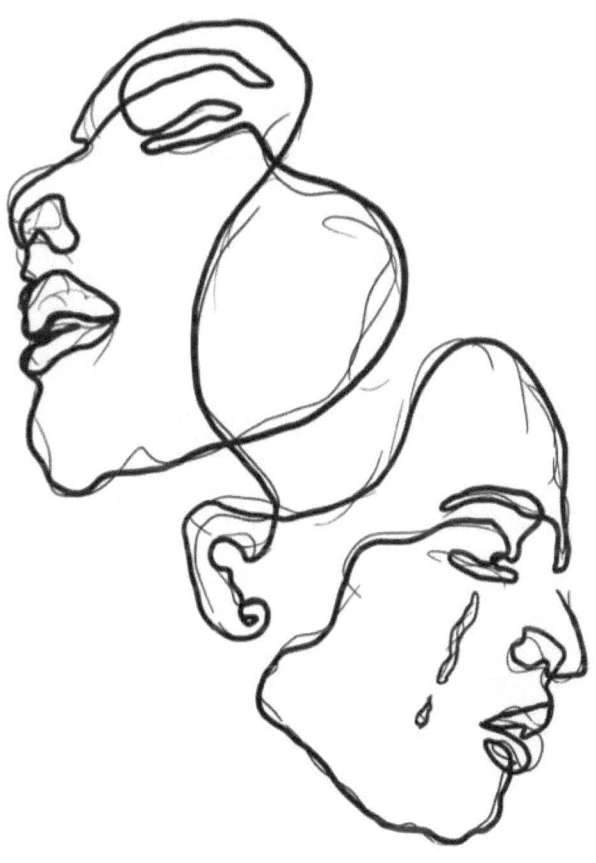

Borderline
by Lena-Marie Plath

Genes

Somewhere between a blessing and a curse,
my thankfulness will find its words
to tell you how much I hate and adore
the pieces you shared within my core.

But hating you means hating me too
and I have been, all my life through.
Just to understand we'll never find common ground
I've been trying to climb up that mount-

-ain since crawling age.
Trying to prove that all of it was made
by me and only me and no one helped
yet you still claim ownership.

How is a kid supposed to learn how to walk
from a person that never ran a mile.
Can a child learn how to grow up,
if it was raised by another child.
Is a toddler able to speak the truth,
if it listened to lies throughout its youth.

Now look at you, now look at me.

Just understand how far we've come.

I've known you since beginning of time

and we've still been fighting since day one.

We used to play like we're best friends.

We used to chase and play pretend,

but since you've gone your way, so far,

I cannot really tell who you are.

One more thing you need to know.

One more hug and then I go.

Can't you see how much I've tried,

with all the words I know you lied.

Look at me, just one more time,

remember back then, when it used to be fine.

Just you and me, right at the beach.

You've always been something, no one could not reach.

Now let me speak, sit down and listen,

listen up and let me talk:

I might not be the perfect painting,

nor the fastest in my class.

No more hiding and no more faking.

My genes persist, stand strong and last.

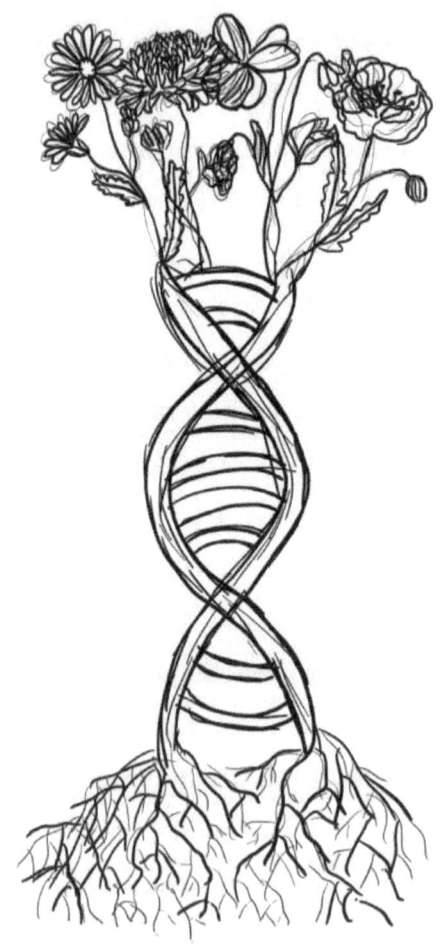

Genes
by Lena-Marie Plath

Intoxication

Stranded somewhere far from home,
the sun, the sky, the beach, I own.
My body's sore from swimming far,
no blood, no break, not even a scar.

I feel relieved with what I left,
my heart is beating in my chest.
The wind blows right through my hair
as we keep running, going nowhere.

Let's build a bridge with sticks and stone.
Cause that is what we know, we own.
Let's build a bridge, forever strong.
Chasing ghosts and then be gone.

I'm lost, I'm lost in paradise,
so stuck, so stuck, I'm paralyzed.
I'm lost, I'm lost in paradise,
my paradise, right in your eyes.

Let's lose ourselves right where we stand,
don't need no one, just grab my hand,
chasing dreams in paradise
I'm lost, I'm lost, right in your eyes.

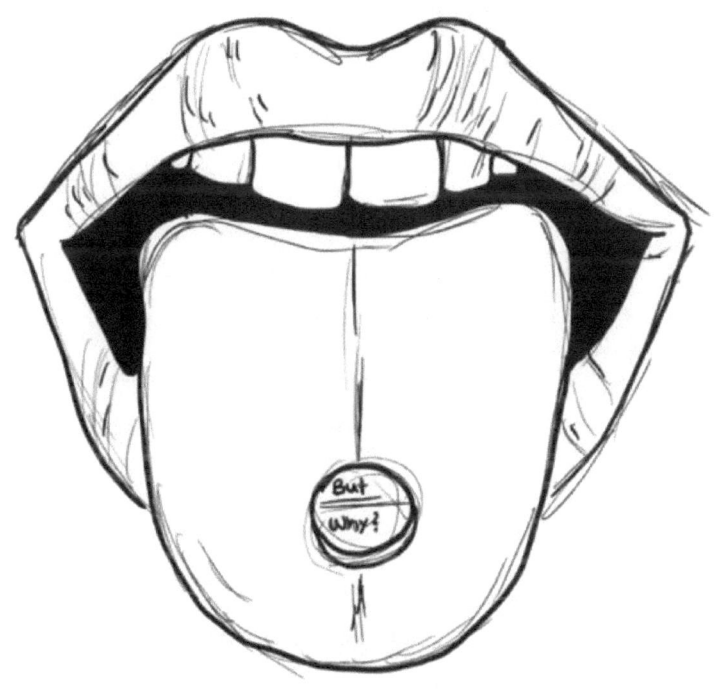

Intoxication
by Lena-Marie Plath

Attention Deficit Disorder

Let me begin this poem with a thought.

Or a couple ideas, or maybe a good way to …

Never mind or never minding?

Mining my ideas like miners in a cave,

caving in, enclosed by a field of boulders.

Stuck.

Light.

My way out.

Starting, beginning, looking around.

Inhaling a scent or enjoying a view and …

Wow… just got stuck in the moment with thousands of things

to do.

But nothing in my hand to begin. Still

I've been searching for something that is hard to find.

In my mind. Buried deep behind an idea.

I feel like a magpie in a silverware store.

Storing or guarding all my precious medals.

Metals made of silver and gold.

Golden like the sun in the desert.

Deserting my ideas to write a good way to start.

Starting to reach for the sky,

In a silverware store, like magpie.

Fly little bird, fly all the way up and

don't get distracted on your way to the sun.

The golden sun that spreads its rays to enlighten …

miners in a cave?

It's so hard to keep one bird in your hand

 while ten thousand pigeon's scatter.

Attention Deficit Disorder
by Lena-Marie Plath

Body Dysmorphia

"You are not enough."
sings the voice in my head, while
the scale proves that I am not only losing this battle.

I am faking my smile and painting my hair.
Whilst knowing there is no one here
who loves me and protects me from myself.

I am my Nemesis, and my Nemesis is me.
The anger increases the more that I see
myself.
In a reflection or when I hear me talk,
the sound of a blackboard scribbled with chalk.

Life is a game; I never chose to play.
If I dress colorfully, they want me in gray.
The likes compensate the disgust, I imagine to see.
When I enter the room, all eyes are on me.

Stuck in a maze of not fitting in
even though I am trying so hard to be thin.
I want to look in the mirror and say
"with you I can spend the rest of my day"

My heart just screams "you are enough".
But my mind just does not seem to care.
My journey is going to be long and rough.
I need help and I can, that's why I share.

Body Dysmorphia
by Lena-Marie Plath

Remedy

I wonder how my lyrics would change.
If they had been written in a different emotion.
I wonder if my paragraphs sound different,
if only other ears would try to listen.

I wonder how my music sounds,
for people without a single worry.
All I know is that we never know.
It might be all a different story!

When you ask me: why choose such harsh words?
Why not write something nice?
Why pour your heart out with paper and pen?
Why read every line twice?

This might not be the remedy.
Nor the enigma to my soul.
Though taking a sip fuels me with energy
until I feel halfway whole.

My answer is so complex and simple:

It all belongs to me.

'Cause every emotion I have ever felt,

Has its right to be.

Seated at my **table of illnesses**

where every seat's alike.

And I am just a waiter serving,

And my happiness is the price.

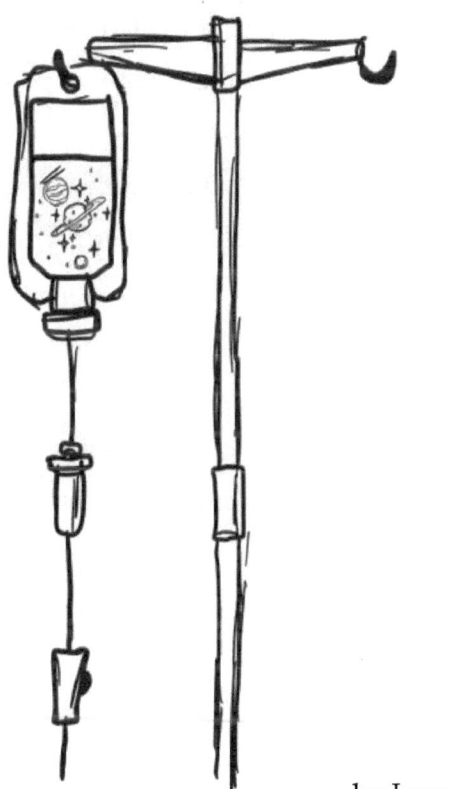

Remedy
by Lena-Marie Plath

Petrichor

Have you ever smelled the scent in the air
on a street or grove or gravelly road?
After declaring that "life is unfair".
Feeling insane, ready to explode.

Nevertheless, you are standing here.
After the storm that devastated entire streets.
Stuck and still filled with fear
read all the way through these paper sheets.

A smell or a scent like a sunrise after the flood
or the feeling of releasing your arm from a cast
after breaking it from playing in the mud
or the days we started breathing without a mask.

Like a vacation or a first kiss.
A nice note from a person you missed.
Words that explain why "you matter".
A gift that makes you feel better.

A stranger greeting while saying "HI"
or the pain from our final "goodbye".

My Petrichor is nothing more and nothing less,

like metaphor in its favorite dress.

To let you smell, oh every scent.

'Cause life offers so much more with a little strength.

If there is one thing, I want you to take away.

It's that the end is inevitable, and your birth had been done.

Your life is so precious, and you are here to stay,

and everything in between those two

is your playground to have some

fun.

Petrichor
by Lena-Marie Plath

Epilog

Kunst kennt weder Geschlecht noch Herkunft oder Sexualität.

Kunst provoziert, zeigt auf, lässt etwas fühlen oder ist aufgrund einer Idee geboren worden. Zwischen "Wahnsinn" und "Brillanz" liegt nur ein Hauch und wenn die Verzweiflung, Freude oder die Emotion im Allgemeinen schwer zu fassen ist, können manchmal tausend Wörter nicht beschreiben, was einem durch den Kopf geht.

Emotionen machen das Leben bunt und ähnlich wie bei der "rosaroten Brille", können Gefühle die Perspektiven verfärben. Gefühle sind persönlich, individuell und immer berechtigt.

Das Kreieren von „Table of Illnesses" war eine persönliche und lange Reise über viele Jahre der emotionalen Achterbahnfahrt. Einige Menschen haben diese Reise begleitet und ebenso viele sind währenddessen ausgestiegen. Mit diesem Buch erhält man eine Freifahrt von Kummer über Verlust bis hin zur Akzeptanz. Diese erfolgt in Form einer warmen und erschöpften Umarmung.

Jede Strophe, jeder Zeilenbruch und auch jede Darstellung der Texte und Illustrationen sind intendiert und bewusst gewählt – auch wenn es die Syntax und Lesefluss beeinflussen kann. Ebenso spielt das Leben nun einmal.

Vielen Dank an alle, die meine Reise begleitet und mit mir beendet haben.

Dein Janus Brodersen

Epilogue

Art knows neither gender nor origin or sexuality.

Art provokes, reveals, makes you feel something or is born out of an idea. There is only a breath between "madness" and "brilliance" and when despair, joy or emotion in general is difficult to grasp, sometimes a thousand words cannot describe what is going through your head.

Emotions make life colorful and similar to "rose-colored glasses", feelings can tint perspectives. Feelings are personal, individual, and always justified.

Creating "Table of Illnesses" has been a personal and long journey over many years of emotional rollercoaster. Some people have accompanied this journey and just as many have dropped out along the way. With this book, you get a free ride from grief to loss to acceptance. This comes in the form of a warm and exhausted embrace.

Every verse, every line break and every representation of the text and illustrations are intentional and deliberately chosen - even if it can affect the syntax and flow of reading. That's the way life works.

Many thanks to all those who have accompanied and completed my journey with me.

Yours, Janus Brodersen

Zeitfracht Medien GmbH
Ferdinand-Jühlke-Straße 7
99095 Erfurt, Deutschland
produktsicherheit@kolibri360.de